Super
SUBMARINES

To Edward Stansfield (aka Ed) with bubbles – T.M.
For My – A.P.

First published 2006 by Kingfisher
This edition published 2013 by Macmillan Children's Books
an imprint of Pan Macmillan,
a division of Macmillan Publishers Ltd
20 New Wharf Road, London N1 9RR
Associated companies throughout the world
www.panmacmillan.com

ISBN: 978-1-4472-1268-3

Text copyright © Tony Mitton 2006
Illustrations copyright © Ant Parker 2006
Moral rights asserted.

5 7 9 8 6 4

A CIP catalogue record for this book is available from the British Library.

Printed in China

Super SUBMARINES

Tony Mitton
and
Ant Parker

MACMILLAN CHILDREN'S BOOKS

A submarine's a kind of boat
that dives beneath the sea.

Below the waves is such a strange
and wondrous place to be.

To travel down it takes in water till its tanks are full –

the weight of water gives the submarine
a downward pull.

When it's underwater
the propeller makes it go.
The hydroplanes can tilt to steer it
up or down, like so.

The rudder also steers the sub
and turns it left or right.
Computers help to navigate –
down deep there's not much light.

The periscope can poke above
the waves to peer around,

but further down, the submarine
depends on sonar sound.

The sonar sends a signal out –
a special kind of bleep,

which bounces back to help them guess
what's out there in the deep.

A submarine needs crew
to keep it running night and day.

The crew need living quarters,
where they eat and rest and play.

Submersibles are different subs
that probe the deepest ocean.
Down that far it's still and dark.
There's hardly any motion.

But even there submersibles
discover deep-sea creatures,
which glow or carry lanterns
and have very funny features.

Submersibles are used to rescue
divers, or explore.
They sometimes salvage sunken wrecks
upon the ocean floor.

They're used to service oil rigs,
lay cables and fix pipes.
Their robot subs have cameras
and arms of many types.

But look! Our sub is rising –
its work below is done.

Very soon the busy crew
will see the sky and sun.

Its ballast tanks have emptied –
they've pushed the water out.

The submarine is back in dock.
"Hooray!" the sailors shout.

Submarine bits

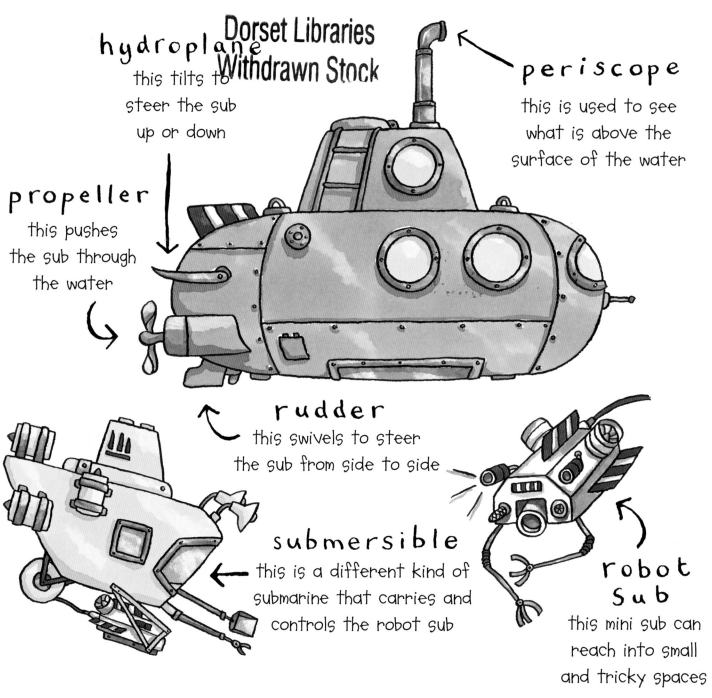

hydroplane
this tilts to
steer the sub
up or down

periscope
this is used to see
what is above the
surface of the water

propeller
this pushes
the sub through
the water

rudder
this swivels to steer
the sub from side to side

submersible
this is a different kind of
submarine that carries and
controls the robot sub

robot sub
this mini sub can
reach into small
and tricky spaces